Praise for the **BAND** **N**

"DJ must have been a fly on the wall of my band room for the last thirty years! I read, smiled, and reflected on people who have all been a part of my band (and my life) over the years. Every once in a while, I found that I was looking in a mirror—and that made me smile too. As you read these poems, you'll see the face and remember the name of each of these people... You'll remember the great times shared with all of the characters...heck, you may even remember the special smell of a well-used band room...then you'll smile too."

—Greg Bimm Director of Bands; Marian Catholic
High School, Chicago Heights, IL

"I'm a band nerd. I admit it. My entire life has been spent playing in, conducting, and teaching bands. I am in this book along with my friends, teachers, and students. And you know what? DJ is right... They are special people, and I like them all. It was a lot of fun to have my life reflected in this book."

—Donald DeRoche, Director of Bands (retired),
1979–2008; DePaul University, Chicago, IL

"Coming from a professional 19th chair band geek who is still searching for her 'ultimate mouthpiece,' I can't think of a better way to cherish the unique inner world of life in the band! These poems prove that participation in school music goes beyond fulfilling an arts credit... It creates a sense of pride, belonging, and humor both onstage and off. Kudos to DJ for creating a hilarious and original work for anyone who has spent even just one day in band class!"

—Amy McCabe Trumpeter/Cornetist, "The
President's Own" United States Marine Band

"*Band Nerds* is a look inside what must be the band room in every school—and a look back at my own inner band nerd. Even years removed, DJ's spot-on humor brings a sheepish smile to my face as I remember those days and all the 'characters' that have been part of MY music history."

—L. Scott McCormick, President and CEO of Music for All, Inc., and the Bands of America and Orchestra America divisions, 1984–2010

"DJ Corchin's book provides a rare, in-depth insight into our nation's band sub-culture, a medium that continues to provide emotional sanctuary for so many of our best and brightest young people. His poetry opens a window for us former band members to reflect fondly upon our school years, while it also garners an opportunity for the rest of the world to understand the powerful force which drives so many of us to success in life."

—Dave Morrison, Illinois Teacher of the Year 2003 and Director of Bands (retired), Prospect High School, Mt. Prospect, IL

"What a KICK! You'll find yourself laughing and sometimes crying at the wonderful words DJ Corchin has articulately and artfully put on paper in this collection of poems. Using the power of poetry, anyone who is in band, was in band, knows someone in band, or knew someone in band will enjoy this book. Whether humorous or harsh, poignant or pathetic, inspiring or irritating—either way DJ hopes you will choose to 'laugh it off.' Helping the reader to rise above the stereotyping that unfortunately sometimes shapes our perceptions and personalities, this book taps into the healthy therapeutic nature of humor to laugh with—and sometimes at—the wonderfully strange world of *Band Nerds*."

—Fran Kick, educational consultant, speaker and author who inspires kids to KICK IT IN®

"Being a member of a band family made the high school years bearable! These poems bring back so many memories as they perfectly describe my time in the flute section. (Thank GOD I switched to bassoon!) This would have been THE book to read when skipping English class...hanging out in the band room of course! A must-read for band students both young and old."

—**Camilla M. Stasa, Director of Participant Relations, Music for All (Bands of America)**

"This fun, humorous, interesting journey through life via membership in the band is a delightful read. These poems joggled my memory and took me back to many wonderful friends, places, and sounds. Change the names and this is my life. At times, we've all stood out, couldn't get it, and/or the entire world was conspiring against us. It's called growing up, and these poems capture the entire exciting roller coaster ride, providing you were fortunate enough to find the band room during your childhood. Enjoy, smile, laugh, and be thankful you were in the band!"

—**Brian Logan, Director of Bands, 1991–2016, Wheeling High School, Wheeling, IL**

BAND NERDS

Awards

NOMINATIONS FROM THE 13TH CHAIR TROMBONE PLAYER

DJ CORCHIN

ILLUSTRATED BY **DAN DOUGHERTY**

sourcebooks
eXplore

Copyright © 2015, 2021 by The phazelFoz Company, LLC
Illustrations by Dan Dougherty
Cover and internal design © 2021 by Sourcebooks
Cover design by Jillian Rahn/Sourcebooks

Sourcebooks and the colophon are registered trademarks of Sourcebooks.

All rights reserved.

The characters and events portrayed in this book are fictitious or are used fictitiously. Any similarity to real persons, living or dead, is purely coincidental and not intended by the author.

This book is a work of humor and intended for entertainment purposes only.

Published by Sourcebooks eXplore, an imprint of Sourcebooks Kids
P.O. Box 4410, Naperville, Illinois 60567-4410
(630) 961-3900
sourcebookskids.com

Originally published in 2015 in the United States of America by The phazelFOZ Company, LLC.

Library of Congress Cataloging-in-Publication Data is on file with the publisher.

Printed and bound in the United States of America.
VP 10 9 8 7 6 5 4 3 2 1

To Ken

TRADITION

There are so many great traditions in music. They connect us with our past so that we can remember our journey. They can make us feel safe as we know that whatever happens, they will always be there. There's comfort in knowing that we can always fall back on the traditions of our musical culture. However, the inherent problem with tradition is that it implies things need to always be done the way they've always been done. Often the only reason given is, "Well, it's tradition." I believe that when tradition is the only reason for having itself, it's time to move on. There should always be purpose in what we do. It's how we move forward. In some cases, tradition is used as an excuse to exclude. That's where we need to step in. If you don't believe a girl should be Drum Major simply because of tradition, not only are you wrong, you're in the way. When traditions get in the way of progress, they are no longer traditions; they're obstacles. Don't be an obstacle. That never turns out well.

AND THE AWARD GOES TO...

Most Intense Saluter

Bassoon Participation Award

Highest Flash

**Most Consecutive Performances without
Cleaning Their Uniform**

Loudest Trumpet

Softest Trumpet

Loudest Flute

Most Exaggerated Story about Almost Dying on the Field

Most Intense Pass-Through

Best Player According to Their Own Parents

"Gets It the Most"

Best Stick Trick

One Year Ago...

Most Improved Player

Current Year

Best Use of Instrument

Most Organized Instrument Locker

Most Innovative Use of Technology

Most Creative Use of Sectional Time

Largest Spit Pool

Largest Spit Pool by a Woodwind

Most Courageous

Most Spectacular Plume

**Humanitarian Award for an Invention
Eliminating a Trombone's Blind Spot**

Straightest Company Front

First Clarinet Section Ever to Be Heard

**Knowing the Most about Music Theory,
but the Least about How Much People Care about
Knowing the Most about Music Theory**

Most in Need of Paper Clips to Straighten

Most Hours Practicing Marching

Highest Drum Major Podium

Oldest Drum Major Podium

Most Improved Flag Work

Least Improved Flag Work

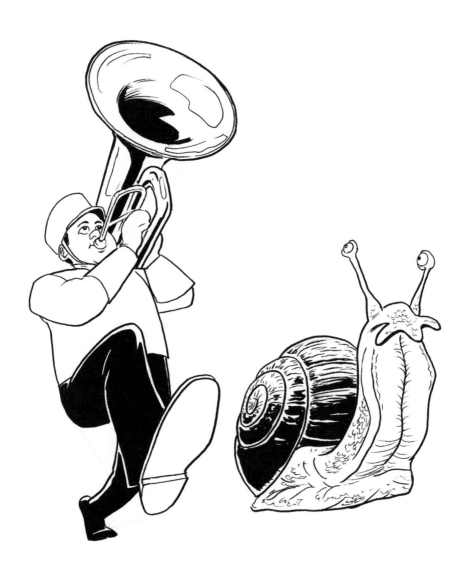

Fastest Person with a Tuba

Person Who Practices the Most but Needs to the Least

Best Drill Written for Oboe

Most Overdone Practice Wear

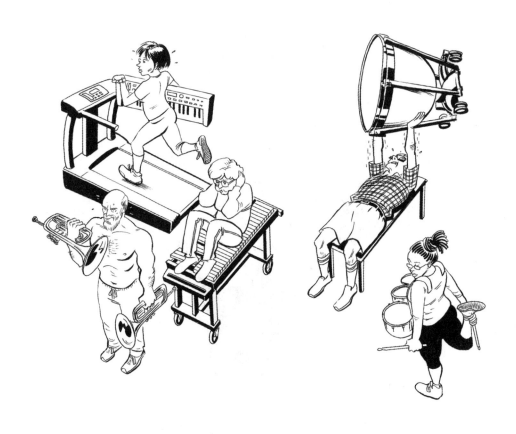

Most Difficult Pit Crew to Qualify for

Most Suped-Up Pit Vehicle

Most Flexible Flute

Best Example of "Just Keep Going"

Hottest Practice Surface

**Most Consecutive Days Wearing Black Jeans and
Old-Timey Paperboy Hat in 90-Degree-Plus Weather**

Most Texts Sent during Rehearsal

Best Solution for the Perfect Horn Angle

**Best Timed "I Needed That" Conversation
in the Band Room after School**

Designated Instrument to Be Left behind in Case of a Fire

Best "Show Face"

Longest Time Standing at Attention

Most Envious

Best Fort Builders

**Parent Who Always Has a Truck Available
to Borrow but Is an Accountant**

Best Uniform Parents

Best Distance-Keeper from Bad Breath

Biggest Knee Bend before the Big Hit

Worst Bus-Packing Job

Director Who Loves Technology the Most

Most Reflective Director Sunglasses

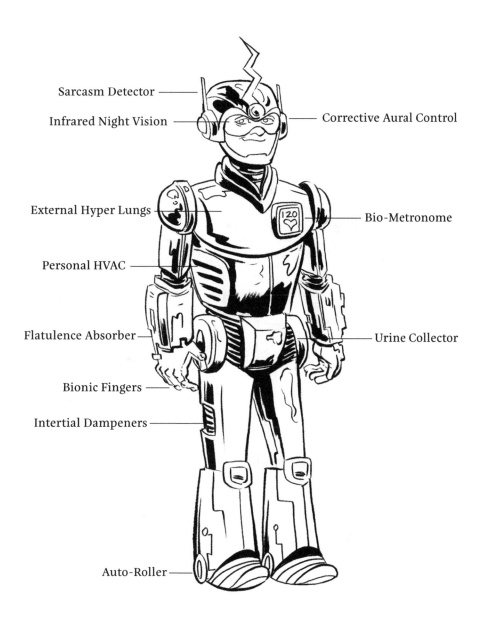

Sarcasm Detector

Infrared Night Vision

Corrective Aural Control

External Hyper Lungs

Bio-Metronome

Personal HVAC

Flatulence Absorber

Urine Collector

Bionic Fingers

Intertial Dampeners

Auto-Roller

Best Uniform

Best Boom That Shakes the Room

Most Upset That Someone Called Star Wars "Star Trek"

Most Amount of Props

Best View

Most More Knowledgeable than Any Judge

Most Intense Counter

Most Likely to Star in Their Own Band Indie Film

**Best "If You Miss Your Spot and We Have to
Run It Again I'm Going to Kill You" Face**

**Person Who Already Assumes They're Going to
Win an Award but the Season Just Started**

Best at Being Able to Spin Anything

Most Frequently Gets the Sousa Case with the Broken Wheel

Most Acrobatic Solo

Most Overzealous Sound Designer

Least Complicated Show

Toughest Sax Player

Most Mallets Used in a Show by One Player

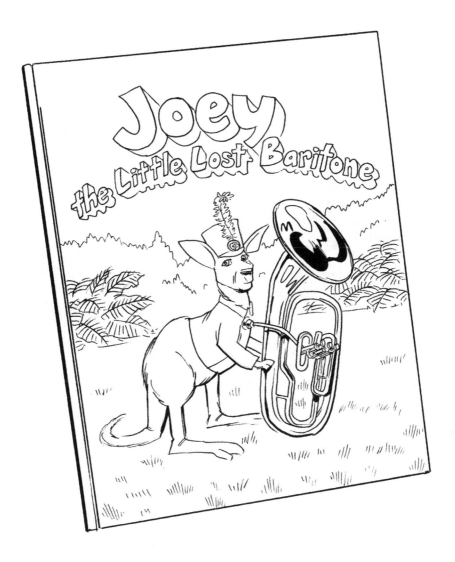

Best Children's Band Book

Calmest Pre-Show Ritual

Weirdest Pre-Show Ritual

Actual Flight Achievement

Best Use of Saber

Latest Time Returning from a Competition

Largest Step Size 1 to 5

Stupid Stereotype Destroyer

Best Dreamer

Best Place to Be

PEACE WITH A WHOLE LOTTA HAIR GREASE.

SEE YA.

DJ CORCHIN, otherwise known in the band world as the 13th Chair, has been involved in music education since learning to play the viola in third grade. And by learning, he means immediately forgetting how to play it the following year when he started on trombone. Growing up in the band world, DJ graduated from DePaul University in Chicago with a degree in music education and immediately did not use it. Instead, he became a featured performer riding a unicycle and playing the trombone in the Tony and Emmy Award–winning Broadway show, *Blast!*, as one does. Shortly after, he became a high school band director developing band nerds for future world domination. When a takeover didn't materialize, he started a career as a children's author writing books about kindness and communication. As one does.

COLLECT ALL THE
BAND NERDS
BOOKS!

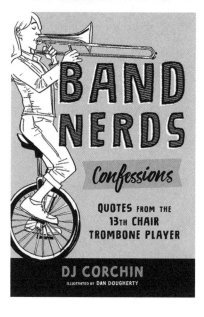